THE
NATURAL
SUPERIORITY
OF THE left
HANDER

THE NATURAL SUPERIORITY OF THE left HANDER

James T. de Kay

ANGUS & ROBERTSON PUBLISHERS

ANGUS & ROBERTSON PUBLISHERS

Unit 4, Eden Park, 31 Waterloo Road,
North Ryde, NSW, Australia 2113, and
16 Golden Square, London W1R 4BN,
United Kingdom

First published in the United States
by M. Evans and Company, Inc.
as The Left-Handed Book in 1966
and The Natural Superiority of the Left-Hander in 1979
This combined edition first published in Australia
by Angus & Robertson Publishers in 1986
First published in the United Kingdom
by Angus & Robertson (UK) Ltd in 1986
Reprinted 1988, 1990

Copyright © 1966, 1979 by James T. de Kay
Copyright © this adaptation 1986
by James T. de Kay
Published by arrangement with
M. Evans and Company, Inc., New York

National Library of Australia
Cataloguing-in-publication data.

De Kay, James T.
    The natural superiority of the left-hander.
    ISBN 0 207 15435 X

    1. Left and right-handedness — Caricatures and
    cartoons. 2. American wit and humour. Pictorial.
    I. Title.

741.5'973

Printed in the United Kingdom

Dedicated to Alexander the Great, Benjamin Franklin, Babe Ruth, Hans Holbein, Betty Grable, Rock Hudson, Peter Lawford, Rudy Vallee, Joanne Woodward, Dick Van Dyke, Judy Garland, Charlemagne, Pablo Picasso, King George VI, Lord Nelson, Joan of Arc, Napoleon Bonaparte, Billy the Kid, Rod Laver, Martina Navratilova, John McEnroe, Jimi Hendrix and half the Beatles (Paul and Ringo), who are all left-handed, and to Gareth de Kay, who is not.

One person in ten is a left-hander. And all of them think they're sort of special.

Which is probably true . . .

No kidding. Anywhere you look, left-handedness is something of a rarity.
Even most plants are right-handed. Honeysuckle is one of the few climbing plants that twines to the left.

It could be that the only case where left-handers are in the majority is among gorillas. Their left arms outweigh their right, which may indicate a slight left-handed bias. But that's only speculation.

As far as human beings are concerned, as we know from cave drawings, in the early days there were plenty of right-handers, but there were plenty of left-handers, too.

If Neanderthal men were exclusively right-handed, they would have invented right-handed tools, correct? Instead, they invented **ambidextrous** tools, suitable for either hand:

hammers,

saws,

axes,

pails,

pottery,

Obviously, a lot of left-handed Neanderthals helped design these clever innovations.

knives,

cups,

flutes,

chairs,

bows & arrows,

tables.

Throughout much of ancient history, the left-handers had equal rights:

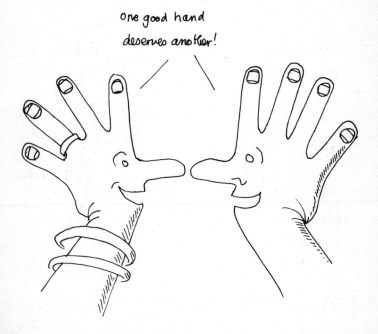

one good hand deserves another!

This was even true in writing . . .

The Egyptians didn't feel they had to write left to right. They wrote up, down, left **or** right, depending on whim.

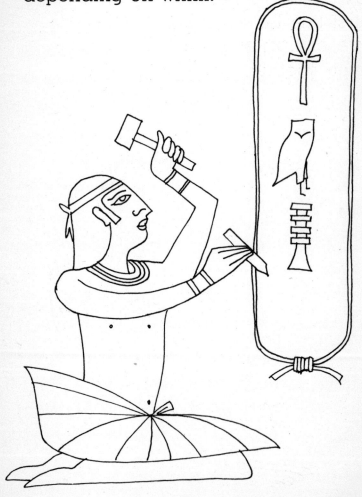

The Greeks wrote BOUSTRO-
PHEDON style, with each line
alternating down the page, like an
ox plowing a field:
first line left to right,
next line right to left,
then another left to right
etc.etc.

The Chinese, even to this day, write in vertical columns from right to left, which would indicate a slightly left-handed preference.

B IBLICAL NOTE: The Israelites
were twice defeated by a
Benjaminite army of "700 picked
men who were left-handed".

Wow! And there's 699 more right behind him!

Actually, it was the Romans who made up all the rules against left-handers. They were the most militantly right-handed people in history.

R omans invented the right-handed handshake . . .

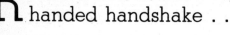

NERO & PROSPER ITY

. . . the fascist salute . . .

ABCDEFGHI
KLMNOPQ
RSTVWXYZ

. . . and that left to right alphabet
that still causes a lot of trouble:

The Roman word for **right** was:

DEXTER

Their word for **left** was:

SINISTER

Is it any wonder left-handedness went out of style?

In the Dark Ages, after the Roman Empire collapsed, a lot of people gave up reading, writing, shaking hands and saluting, and went back to being left-handed. Once again, the tools invented in this period reflect a general ambidextrality.

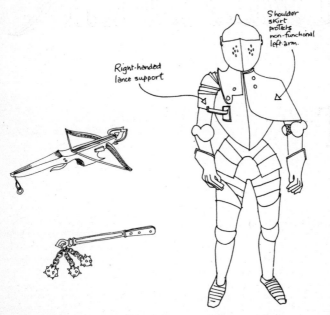

Shoulder skirt protects non-functional left arm.

Right-handed lance support

But by the Middle Ages left-handers were out in the cold. Even suits of armour were invariably right-handed.

M IDDLE EASTERN FOOTNOTE:
The Arabs have always
insisted you eat with your right
hand. This taboo isn't really
directed against left-handers, but
stems solely from certain social
problems that arise where water is
scarce. Some time back in history,
they decided that the left hand
should be reserved for certain
hygienic purposes, the intensely
personal nature of which made that
hand particularly unsuitable for the
communal dinner pot.

To show their impartiality, Arabs
write left-handedly:

Today, we're right back where we were with the Romans. Just about everything's right-handed. Take jet planes. The pilot sits on this side so he can operate the all-important centre control panel.

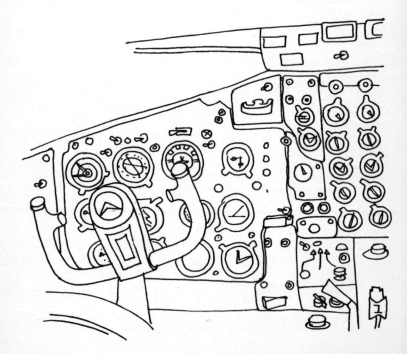

But what if the pilot's left-handed? He'd be more efficient on this side, but he's not allowed to sit here. Is this the safest possible arrangement?

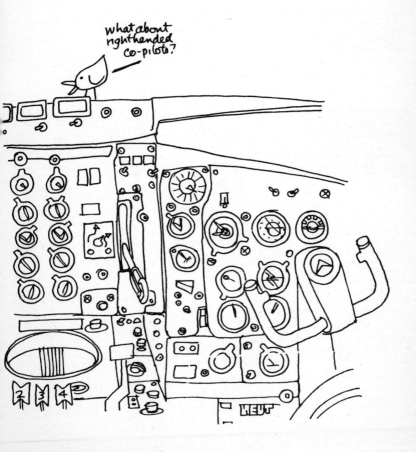

what about righthanded co-pilots?

That long-ago bias against left-handers is still with us.

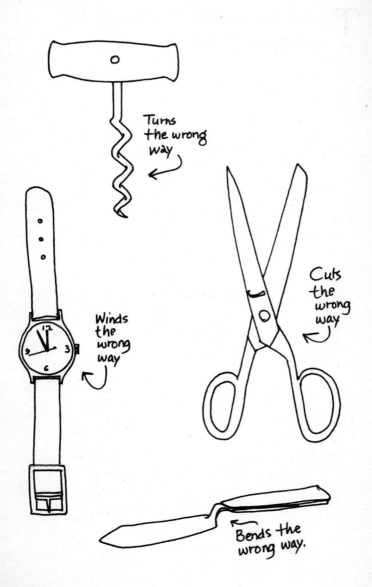

Turns the wrong way

Winds the wrong way

Cuts the wrong way

Bends the wrong way.

But for some reason not quite clear, left-handers make fantastic tennis players. At any

given time, about 40% of the top pros are left-handed . . . people like Rod Laver, Jimmy Connors, Manuel Orantes, Guillermo Villas, Martina Navratilova, etc.

Swimming also favours left-handers. Neurologists have shown they adjust more readily to underwater vision. Mark Spitz, the American who won seven Olympic gold medals, was, as you might expect, left-handed.

But polo is another story. It's actually **against the rules** to play left-handed.

And that even goes for the left-handed Prince Charles.

Jimi Hendrix was neither rich nor important, but he became both by beating right-handers at their own game. He restrung his guitar so he could play it left-handed.

Where does left-handedness come from? Is it inherited? Maybe.

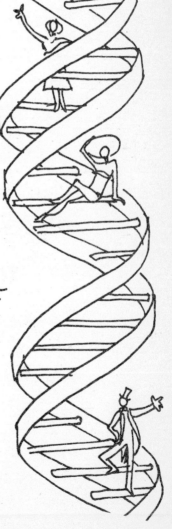

But... can something as rigorously right-handed as the DNA helix actually transmit left-handedness?

One indication that left-handed-ness is genetic comes from Scotland's Kerr family.

For centuries the Kerrs have been famous for the large number of left-handers they produce.

They even gave their castles left-handed staircases so they'd be easy to defend.

At one time, American Indians may have been the world's largest single population of left-handers. There's evidence that one in three was left-handed.

The Incas thought left-handedness was lucky. One of their great chiefs was LLOQUE YUPANQUI, which means left-handed.

Inca-dinka-doo.

We know that if both parents are left-handed, 50% of the kids will be left-handed too.

B ut if both parents are right-
handed, only 2% of the kids
will be left-handed.

Older mothers are more likely to produce left-handed children than younger mothers.

There's a high incidence of left-handedness in twins, but it's rare to find both left-handed.

Some experts claim they can spot a left-hander in infancy. The whorl of their hair, it is said, will twist counter-clockwise.

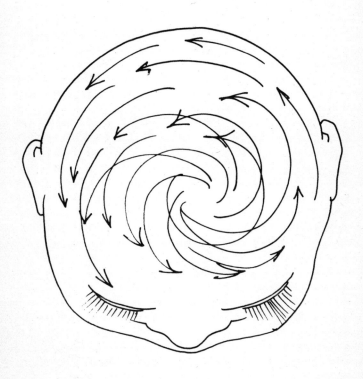

Virtually all pediatricians will agree that if a child has a preference for the left hand, it will show up by age five.

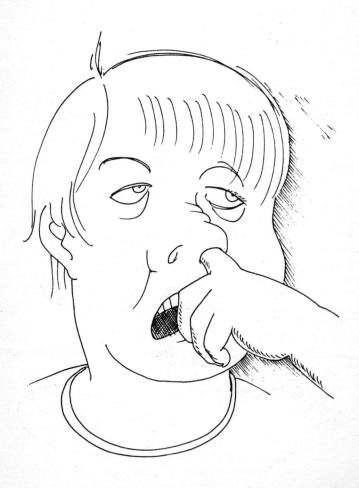

Researcher Theodore Blau recommends this test. Using each hand in turn, draw X's, then circle them. If you draw the circles anti-clockwise you're left-handed (he says).

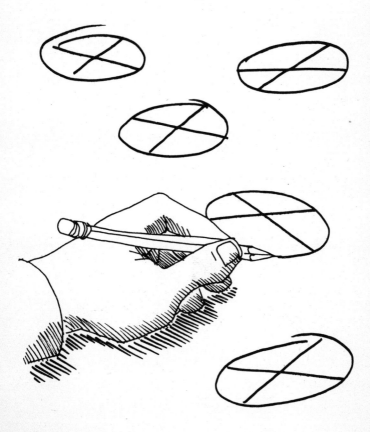

The New England Journal of Medicine suggests you can tell you're left-handed if the base of your left thumbnail is wider and squarer than the right.

Well, at least everyone agrees left-handers are special. But are they specially good?

Or specially bad?

To find out, we must enter a very strange world . . . the world of the human brain . . . a shadowy place of surprises and contradictions, only partially

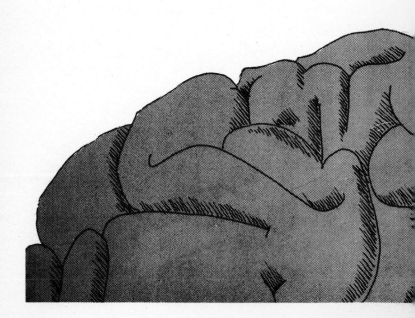

mapped and imperfectly
understood. But we know it holds
the key to the secret of left-
handedness.

The brain is made up of two very different hemispheres. We need both, but for different reasons, since each has its own functions . . .

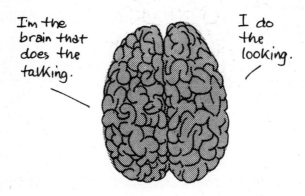

I'm the brain that does the talking.

I do the looking.

its own personality . . .

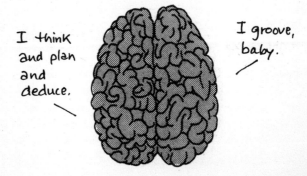

I think and plan and deduce.

I groove, baby.

its own specialties . . .

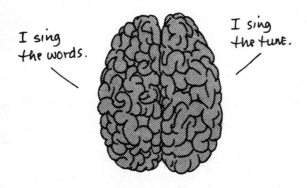

I sing the words.

I sing the tune.

and most significantly, in reference to the subject under consideration, its own hand.

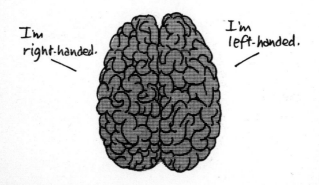

I'm right-handed.

I'm left-handed.

Because they have such different points of view, the "thinking"

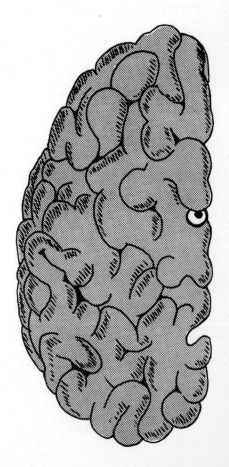

Hey! I'm in charge here! It stands to reason! I'm the responsible one!

and "feeling" hemispheres compete
for dominance.

Why— don't you blow it out your nose?

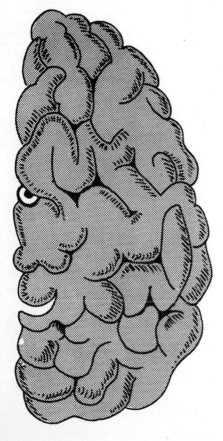

G enerally speaking, people with a dominant "thinking" brain become right-handed.

It seems only reasonable!

While those with a dominant "feeling" brain become left-handed.

You might expect a right-hander to be verbal, analytical, and good at maths.

So I unload United Federal in a short position, while recognizing that Amalgamated could crossruff my ITD before Uncle Sam got his greedy mitts on it...

A nd a left-hander to be intuitive, and mystical, with a strong visual sense. Which is exactly the case.

That's the third time today Cauthen's worn green silks.

In politics, maybe this is why cold, heartless conservatives are called right-wingers.

Commie!

And why dreamy, bleeding heart liberals are called left-wingers.

Fascist!

A lot of hard evidence shows that most left-handers—because they are dominated by a different kind of brain—are a distinctly different kind of people.

They literally think differently,
even when solving the same
problem as a right-hander.
Right-handers adapt comfortably to
abstractions.
But left-handers tend to translate
everything into visual imagery.

R ight-handers tend to think
lineally, linking their ideas in
logical order.

L eft-handers are more apt to think holistically, skipping over the details.

Which explains why so many creative people have been left-handed.

Edward R. Murrow

H.G. Wells

Pablo Picasso

Ronald Searle

Anthony Newley

Leonardo

Michaelangelo

Murray Skurnik

Paul Williams

Jim Bishop

Peter Benchley

Paul Klee

Milton Caniff

Hans Holbein

Clarence Darrow

And why left-handers seem almost to dominate show business.

Greta Garbo

Charlie Chaplin

Marcel Marceau

Glen Campbell

Telly Savalas

Richard Pryor

George Burns

Lenny Bruce

Shirley MacLaine

Rex Harrison

Michael Landon

Jim Henson

Robert De Niro

Marilyn Monroe

And perhaps most interesting of all, it helps explain one of the more intriguing statistics of the space age. When NASA went searching for the kind of imaginative, super-reliable, multi-talented people they would need to explore the moon . . .

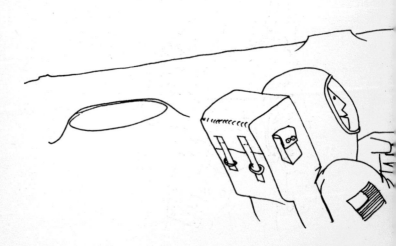

. . . one out of every four Apollo astronauts turned out to be left-handed—a figure

250%

greater than statistical probability.

Something's not right here!

Far from being society's misfits, data like this suggests that left-handers are almost a different species. Who knows? Maybe they're the next step up in evolution.

In any case, we now know why left-handers have always believed they were special.

In their hearts, they know they're right.